Parent's Guide

Written by James H. Ritchie, Jr., Ed.D.

Nan Zoller, Editor/Contributor

Created by God

Tweens, Faith, and Human Sexuality

Parent's Guide

ISBN 978-1-426-70041-5

Dr. James H. Ritchie, Jr., Writer
Nan Zoller, Editor/Contributor
Marcia Stoner, Supervising Editor
Marjorie M. Pon, Editor, Church School Publications
Karen Scholle, Production Editor
Keitha Vincent, Designer

Art Credits:
Cover Design Concept: Ken M. Strickland
Pages 6, 10, 12, 22, 25: Liquid Library

09 10 11 12 13 14 15 16 17 18—10 9 8 7 6 5 4 3 2 1
MANUFACTURED IN THE UNITED STATES OF AMERICA

PACP00457031-01

Created by God

Tweens, Faith, and Human Sexuality

Parent's Guide

Written by James H. Ritchie, Jr., Ed.D.
Nan Zoller, Editor/Contributor

Contents

We're in This Together

Welcome

You are the parents of a tween, nearly a teenager. This came kind of fast, didn't it? And now it's time to make sure your son or daughter is fully informed about sexuality, his or her body, and God's wonderful plan for us. It seems just weeks ago you were the parent of a newborn!

The good news is that you are not alone. By participating in *Created by God,* you are forming a partnership with your church and family of faith. That's a great connection! Through this experience, you and your daughter or son will share increased open communication for years to come, and your tween will have correct sexuality information presented within Christian values and an emphasis on abstinence.

This isn't the first sexuality information your child has received. You have been your child's primary sexuality education since birth! You haven't talked about this? No matter! All parents are providing sexuality education whether or not they have intentionally embraced that task. Some parents are willing and able to assist their sons and daughters in assimilating accurate anatomical and reproductive information and in adopting healthy attitudes, but most often home instruction is the result of simple observation.

From birth, children observe their parents interacting with each other and with other adults.

That's the way they learn how women and men are, their roles, and their "worth," at least according to your family. They observe the similarities and the differences in how parents interact with sons and with daughters, the expectations and the allowed behaviors. Children watch and listen to how parents react to off-color jokes, how they use slang terms for the human body and bodily functions, and how parents react to the presence of stated or implied sexuality in the media. Children listen to language and note parents' level of comfort and discomfort when persons speak in a direct manner about sexuality.

Regardless of the degree, sexuality education is taking place in your home. That's where it starts, for better or for worse. The support of the church—through relationships, resources, and educational opportunities—will strengthen your child's experience of sexuality education and will shape the sexuality understandings for a lifetime.

Getting the Conversation Started

Many parents have not had much experience using proper terminology about bodies and sexuality. Many parents never had anyone talk to them about sex and have done little talking themselves. This can be radically new territory!

Parents who have experienced human sexuality studies with their sons and daughters often comment that the greatest blessing has been the strengthening of communication with their tweens. Some of those conversations are about sex; some aren't. What's important is that parents and tweens are communicating.

Reading *Created by God* together can initiate such conversation. With joint reading, parents know that their children have been exposed to concepts and terminology related to sexuality. The young persons know the same about parents. Not only does everyone know that everyone else knows about sex, they also have opportunities to ask questions. Likewise, following the *Created by God* experience, especially including the closing Parent/Tween session with either the Parent/Tween Directed Conversation or the Fishbowl Activity, tweens and parents recognize that they can talk about this formerly sensitive subject together. You're actually much closer to "the same page" than they had thought!

Join the Team

Involvement in a group study provides a broader information base as well as a wider diversity of perspectives on human sexuality. In entering into group conversation, we recognize that none of us has the answers, nor is one opinion or perspective right. Within the body of Christ there is a broader vision—a vision that is rooted in a common commitment to Christ and a common desire to discover the will of God for all of our human relationships. The Study Leader, Small Group Leaders, and community of parents and tweens will work together to provide one another with new understandings, common experiences, and a revived sense of what it means to say we have been and are being created by God.

Teaching our children about sex and sexuality is not easy—particularly when we wish to do so with an emphasis on Christian values. We believe that the partnership of parents and church, joining together in a special covenant, is the strongest and most effective approach. You, Mom or Dad, are your child's primary mentor when it comes to human sexuality education. The church and *Created by God* are here to help you with your task.

We're Not Isolated

There are some cultural realities: your son or daughter is growing up in a different time and place than you did. Some of it is better, some of it isn't. One part of that reality is that today's tweens develop physically and sexually at earlier ages, although they are still chronologically and emotionally children. Their bodies are becoming capable of and interested in sexual activity long before they reach the markers of social, academic, or financial adulthood. While we want them to delay sexual activity until marriage, it is a very difficult expectation. At the same time, for tweens we firmly urge abstinence.

Besides the media invasion of our households, tweens today have less supervised time, more access to outside connections, and certainly more communication means. There are many voices telling tweens to live only in the "now," that they are ready for sexual activity now (and are abnormal if they aren't sexually active), and that sexual activity is unconnected to relationship or love. While parents often think they are invisible, all studies show that parents still remain the major force in the lives of their tweens and teens. Therefore, don't give your power away! Use your voice in every teachable moment to express your values and expectations. This doesn't have to be lectures, but statements of expectations and comments about the actions of persons in the media and others. In addition, be sure that your lives are positive models for your sons and daughters. They are watching!

Be aware that some studies show a direct relationship between the quality of the father-daughter relationship and the infrequency of teen sexual activity. We can only speculate that a strong positive relationship between mother and son will bring about a son who values and respects females and who is less likely to use them for sexual gratification outside of a relationship. So, rather than decrease time together, be intentional about increasing quality time with your tween.

Why the Church?

Why is the church sponsoring such an event?

How is *Created by God* different from school curriculum?

As God's voice in the world, the church must speak for the biblical understanding that sexuality is not separate from the Christian's life and is God-given, not nasty or evil, shameful or perverse. As that Christian voice, we want to equip, empower, and guide sexuality education for tweens and their parents with a faith-based perspective, teaching Christian value-based tools for adolescence and decision making. We want to strengthen the church and family partnership and to provide correct anatomical information in an atmosphere of respect for God's gift, our bodies. Finally, we want to encourage abstinence before marriage.

We want to present the biblical basis for recognizing God's creative action at the beginning, and that continuing creative action in every birth. We want to affirm God's presence with us in all times of our lives. And we want to cite the promises of forgiveness when we fall short of God's divine plan. The biblical stories and passages that form the foundation for *Created by God* have been chosen to underscore the goodness of God's human creation, the impact of disobedience, and God's desire that we live in an intimate relationship with God and with one another. You'll find a listing of those Scriptures at the end of this guide, as well as an overview.

Lastly, *Created by God* is different from school curriculum and the like because boys and girls are together for every session. Doesn't that make them uneasy? Will they be free to ask questions? Aren't they embarrassed? No, yes, and no. At this age, girls

and boys are used to learning together. And they are interested in learning how the other half's body works. We sometimes tell them they need to understand the other because they'll likely marry one of those! Our experience shows that tweens are free to ask all kinds of questions, first in the Question Box and later out loud in every session. While there may be some giggles at first, the embarrassment fades quickly and curiosity takes over.

What Will They Learn?

What will they learn? Will they like it?

Through the *Created by God* experience, tweens will learn correct anatomical and reproductive terms and exactly how sexual intercourse and birth happens. They will learn that healthy married people are sexually active for their entire lives (and they'll deduce that means you, too!). They will learn that with adolescent hormones comes sexual attraction and drives that we must learn to control, but which when used correctly can bring great joy. And tweens will learn that abstinence is right at this time.

We have rarely found a tween who wants to give up a ball game, a school dance, or even just a night at home to come to church and hear about sex. You can tell them all the reasons why this is important, that they will get valuable information, that their friends are attending, that there will be lots of activities. All that is true, but you likely will still have resistance. Ultimately you may simply have to be the parent and insist that this isn't optional. Remember that your son's or daughter's well-being could very well hang in the balance. Our experience shows that even the most reluctant tweens appreciate the experience (although they won't always admit it!).

Finally, be sure that your child knows what he or she is coming to, and that you are aware of the contents and fully support this study.

Are Tweens Ready for This?

Yes and no. They want to know, but don't want to ask. They want to know about their own bodies and the bodies of the other gender. They want someone to separate the truth from the fiction, because, as there has always been, there's a lot of misinformation. They don't want to be left in the "dark" of ignorance. At the same time, they will likely not retain all that they hear. They will retain what they can and need for now. And they will have their student book, increased communication with their parents, and an enduring relationship with at least one Small Group Leader to consult when they need to.

Some parents fear that tweens will be tempted to become sexually active now that they have these newly acquired understandings. Our experience shows that tweens usually receive this information with an "oh, gross" comment. In other words, cognitively they want the information, but physically and sexually they aren't anywhere near ready for the experience.

They're on the Grow

Adolescence compresses the greatest amount of physical change a person experiences into the shortest period—more change in less time than what takes place during infant development. Tweens are predictably unpredictable. Mood swings and energy fluctuations are both typical and part of what makes them special. And because that's a lot of growing and changing, tweens have spells of lethargy amidst bursts of energy.

Everyone's adolescence happens at a different rate. On walking into a group of tweens, one is struck by the amazing differences, not just between boys and girls but among boys and among girls. Size is the most obvious variable, but also remarkable are levels of physical, intellectual, emotional, social, and spiritual maturity. For example, among girls, some have been menstruating for a year or more; some have begun breast development. Among boys, some are beginning growth spurts; some are experiencing voice changes. At a time when tweens most want to blend in, their bodies and their behaviors betray them. That is the very thing they have in common!

Overall, studies show that tweens are maturing faster and faster, starting the process six months or more earlier than the previous generation. And, there are also false signs of "maturity" like clothing, language, and exposure to explicitly sexual images that were formerly restricted to adults.

Beyond Their Years

Tweens seem like children in one instant and like miniature adults within seconds. And we sometimes mistake a semi-sophisticated veneer for maturity. On the surface they seem old beyond their years, partly as a result of their exposure to information and marketing of all kinds. They are eager to dress like older teens and experiment with "adult" language.

But exposure and experimentation do not qualify a person for adulthood. In spite of what tweens see and hear of a sexual nature, we cannot conclude that they have also learned to process that information into a complete picture. Both girls and boys are generally better informed about their bodies than were previous generations, in part because of more emphasis on sexuality education, the reality of AIDS, the rise in STD (Sexually Transmitted Disease) rates, and the incidence of teen pregnancy. But girls remain largely uninformed about boys, boys remain uninformed about girls, and both girls and boys are curious about the other gender.

Most young persons still depend on their peers for sexuality information, which results in a pooling of ignorance, as it always has. Yes, tweens are exposed to information and images their parents never saw, but when it comes to the "Three R's" of reproduction, relationships, and responsibilities, young persons still have a lot to learn. Although their world is expanding, tweens' need and desire for parental guidance does not decrease. They want to know where their parents stand, and continue to look to parents to say "no" when they are afraid their own refusal to do something will end up in peer rejection.

Will they ask you questions you don't want to answer? Possibly. Here are some ways you can prepare for difficult questions:

- Read the student book carefully to familiarize yourself with anatomical terms and the approach of the text.
- Be informed (as much as possible) about your son's or daughter's school culture.
- Think carefully now about your own values and what you want to teach your tween.

Think in advance about how you want to answer questions about your own early sexual experiences. How much is too much information? What is appropriate information for now? For later? When should discretion prevail over full disclosure? We urge you to think this through before you are asked. Remember that these are pre-teens and this is not the one-and-only conversation on this subject, but the way you answer can close the door or keep it open for further questions. These are still children in many ways. In that regard, you may choose to say that there are some things that only married persons do or discuss together. However, don't dodge questions. Be aware that the level of conversational intimacy parents establish with their children will make it easier for those children to confide in their parents.

Sensitive Issues

Many parents want to know what will be said about certain sensitive issues. Our first response is that the *Created by God* speaks from Holy Scripture and The Social Principles of The United Methodist Church. We acknowledge that not all people of faith—nor all United Methodists—agree, just as there is not agreement among medical researchers and ethicists. So we will describe the sensitive issues as clearly as possible, then apply scriptural teachings and the church's statement. We urge you to continue these conversations within your family so that your specific values are heard.

Having said that, these are three of the issues about which questions are asked:

- Abortion is the deliberate ending of a pregnancy by medical means. Abortion is legal in most states, with restrictions regarding the length of the pregnancy (usually up to 3 months) and parental consent for minors. Some people regard abortion as murder. Others work to make abortions unnecessary through abstinence campaigns and birth control use. The United Methodist Church says, in part, "*The beginning of life and the ending of life are the God-given boundaries of human existence.... Our belief in the sanctity of unborn human life makes us reluctant to approve abortion.... We recognize tragic conflicts of life with life that may justify abortion, and in such cases we support the legal option of abortion under proper medical procedures.... We cannot affirm abortion as an acceptable means of birth control, and we unconditionally reject it as a means of gender selection.*" (For more see *The Book of Discipline 2008*, Paragraph #161.J, pages 105–106.)

- Contraception is using deliberate means to prevent pregnancy. In some faith traditions, any means of contraception is contrary to the church's teachings. In others, birth control in various forms is accepted and approved as the means to limit family size and to best provide for the children of a family. There is public debate about the age at which young people should receive contraceptive devices and medications without parental notification. We advocate abstinence until marriage, although we generally describe several means of birth control, including sterilizations.
- Homosexuality is sexual attraction to someone of the same gender. We find that children know that word but do not know heterosexuality, so we deliberately define both. In keeping with medical research, we say that there is no conclusive information on why a person is homosexual. We acknowledge that some people of faith see homosexuality as a chosen sin, while others believe homosexuality is not a matter of choice. We emphasize that persons are "good" or "bad" because of what they say and do, not because of their sexual orientation. In other words, a person is neither "bad" or "good" because of gender identification. Further, we discourage rejection or taunting of homosexual persons, and we discourage verbal attacks using slang words for homosexuals.

Knowing that in puberty tweens are experiencing many hormonal shifts and new feelings, we are careful to recognize that some tweens may wonder if they are homosexual and begin to either feel alienated from family and church or to feel pressure from the culture to "come out." We discourage sexual activity of any kind until persons have found a life partner (marriage).

Ultimately, we rely on the words of The United Methodist Social Principles which say that "all persons are of sacred worth" (*The Book of Discipline 2008*, Paragraph #4 Article 4, page 22).

In all the years of leading *Created by God* events, these statements have sufficed.

You'll be able to ask your Study Leader questions about other sensitive issues.

Importance of Full Participation

Created by God is six tightly packed sessions. Every activity is focused on learning; there is no fluff. Therefore, it is imperative that you and your son or daughter attend every session designed for you. Your participation not only gives you information: it sets an example of your participation in sexuality education. Your tween's participation means she or he gets all the information that his or her friends do.

Sometimes there will be conflicts with sports or other activities. Resist the urge to say, "It's just an hour away for an important game." That hour, when you add travel time, means at least two. And, you demonstrate to your child that ball is more important than this experience. We urge you to clear your calendar or consider participating in the next *Created by God*.

Now It's Time

Remember, sexuality education has been happening since your tween first came home from the hospital as an infant. You—along with the church as your partner—are now moving to another chapter in that education. Your tween is ready, and this can't wait. We hope that *Created by God* will support and enrich your family's Christian journey through the challenges of sexuality exploration.

Created by God Overview

Session 2

- Welcome
- Autograph Collection
- "Untangle It" Game
- Whale Story
- Sing
- Introduce the Question Box
- Jesus in Jerusalem
- "Name That Change"
- Writing of Questions and Looking at Books
- Puberty and Adolescence
- The First Creation and Your Creation Craft, Biblical Study
- Respond to the Question Box
- Closing

Session 3

- Welcome
- Adam and Eve
- Language
- Anatomy in Common
- External Reproductive Systems
- Respond to the Question Box
- Internal Reproductive Systems
- Concept of Intimacy and Biblical Foundation
- Small-Group Review
- Closing

Session 4

- Welcome
- Respond to the Question Box
- Reminders of Concepts
- Female Growth and Development
- Male Growth and Development
- Create Male and Female Montages
- Dating, Falling in Love, Marriage
- Review Game
- Song and Closing

Session 5

- Welcome
- Reminders Regarding Marriage
- Love and Sexual Intercourse
- Conception, Fetal Development, and Childbirth
- Respond to the Question Box
- Important Issues:
  - Abstinence
  - Abuse, Rape
  - Birth Control
  - Heterosexuality, Homosexuality
  - Masturbation
  - Oral Sex
  - Internet, Chat Rooms, Phone Sex, Sexting
  - Pornography
  - Pregnancy—Planned/Unplanned
  - STDs and AIDS
  - Question Box and Referral to Book
  - Closing

Parents and Tweens Together
Session 6

- Welcome
- Reproduction Game
- Intimacy Skit
- Parent/Tween Directed Conversation (or Fishbowl Activity)
- Response Forms
- Litanies of Love
- Closing With Song, Scripture, and Blessing

A Biblical Foundation for *Created by God*

The biblical stories and passages that form the foundation for *Created by God* have been chosen to underscore the goodness of God's human creation, the impact of disobedience, and God's desire that we live in an intimate relationship with God and with one another.

In the *Created by God* student book, you will find the following references:

- Genesis 1—Creation: God's plan for us/created in God's image.
- Genesis 2:15–25—God's response to Adam's need for companionship/man and woman become one flesh/created for intimacy.
- Genesis 3—Adam and Eve's act of disobedience.
- Psalm 8:3-5—Human beings created a little lower than God.
- Psalm 139:13–16a—God created every part of me.
- Proverbs 5:18-19—Love and joy in marriage.
- Ecclesiastes 3:1—A time for everything.
- Song of Solomon 2:16a—Union of those in love.
- Mark 12:28-31—Love God, love your neighbor as yourself.
- Luke 10:25-37—The Good Samaritan.
- Luke 2:41-52—Jesus increased in wisdom, in years, and in divine and human favor.
- 1 Corinthians 13:4a—Love is patient.
- 1 Corinthians 13:11—Putting an end to childish ways.
- Galatians 3:28—No male or female, all are one in Christ Jesus.
- Philippians 4:8—Fill your mind with positive ways.
- 1 John 4:20-21—Love God, love your brothers and sisters.

The following passages are used in the sessions for a *Created by God* study:

- Genesis 1:25-31—God creates every kind.
- Genesis 1:1-3—Wind from God sweeps over.
- Genesis 2:7—God's breath creates a living being.
- Luke 2:41-52—Jesus the adolescent increases in wisdom, in years, and in divine and human favor.
- Genesis 2:4b-9, 15-25—Creation of humans.
- Genesis 3:1-13—Humans' first act of disobedience.
- 1 Corinthians 13:11—Giving up childish ways.
- Luke 10:25-37—The Good Samaritan.
- Psalm 139:13-16—I was created by God.
- Mark 12:30—Love God.
- 1 Corinthians 13:4-8a—Paul's definition of love.
- Ecclesiastes 4:9-12—The value of two over one.
- Philippians 2:1-11—Confess Jesus Christ as Lord.
- Philippians 4:8—Fill your mind with all that is positive.
- Mark 12:29-31—Love God, love your neighbor as yourself.
- Isaiah 40:28-31—Those who wait for the Lord shall renew their strength.

Additional Resources for Parents and Tweens

For Parents:

Before They Ask: Talking About Sex From a Christian Perspective—A Guide for Parents of Children From Birth Through Age Twelve, by Don and Rhoda Preston (Abingdon, 1999).

Beyond the Big Talk: Every Parent's Guide to Raising Sexually Healthy Teens—From Middle School to High School and Beyond, by Debra W. Haffner, M.P.H. (Newmarket Press, 2002).

Everything You Never Wanted Your Kids to Know About Sex (But Were Afraid They'd Ask), by Justin Richardson, M.D. and Mark A. Schuster, M.D., Ph.D. (Three Rivers Press, 2003).

From Diapers to Dating: A Parent's Guide to Raising Sexually Healthy Children—From Infancy to Middle School, by Debra W. Haffner (Newmarket Press, 2004).

The New Speaking of Sex: What Your Children Need to Know and When They Need to Know It, by Meg Hickling, R.N. (Northstone Publishing, Canada, 2005).

The Roller Coaster Years: Raising Your Child Through the Maddening Yet Magical Middle School Years, by Charlene C. Giannetti and Margaret Sagarese (Broadway Books, 1997).

The Tween Years: A Parent's Guide for Surviving Those Terrific, Turbulent, and Trying Times Between Childhood and Adolescence, by Donna G. Corwin (Contemporary Books, 1999).

What Every 21st-Century Parent Needs to Know: Facing Today's Challenges with Wisdom and Heart, by Debra W. Hafner (Newmarket Press, 2008).

Editor's Note: At time of printing, these books were in print. We cannot guarantee continued availability. If unavailable, check your local library.

For Tweens:

Chicken Soup for the Preteen Soul, written and edited by Jack Canfield, Mark Victor Hansen, Patty Hansen, and Irene Dunlap (Health Communications, Inc., 2000).

My Body, My Self for Boys, by Lynda Madaras (Newmarket Press, 1993).

My Body, My Self for Girls, by Lynda Madaras (Newmarket Press, 1993).

The What's Happening to My Body Book for Boys: A Growing Up Guide for Parents and Sons, by Lynda Madaras and Area Madaras (Newmarket Press, 2007).

The What's Happening to My Body Book for Girls: A Growing Up Guide for Parents and Daughters, by Lynda Madaras and Area Madaras (Newmarket Press, 2007).

Too Old for This, Too Young for That! Your Survival Guide for the Middle School Years, by Harriet S. Mosatche, Ph.D. and Karen Unger, M.A. (Free Spirit Publishing, 2000).

Younger Children:

On Your Mark, Get Set, Grow: A "What's Happening to My Body?" Book for Younger Boys, by Lynda Madaras (Ages 8 and up) (Newmarket Press, 2008).

Ready, Set, Grow: A "What's Happening to My Body?" Book for Younger Girls, by Lynda Madaras (Ages 8 and up) (Newmarket Press, 2003).

A Family Ritual for Beginning *Created by God*

Use this ritual if you like to have special words and actions to mark this kind of experience. You will need three candles and matches or a lighter.

Parent(s): *Created by God* is a time for us to remember the child you were not so very long ago. We miss the childlike qualities that are now memories. Light one candle to celebrate the special child who once was you.

Tween: (*Light first candle.*)

Parent(s): *Created by God* is a time for us to learn and grow together. There is so much for you to know as you change and lots of wrong information out there. You are ready for a deeper understanding of how God has created you and how that influences your feelings about yourself, about others, and about God. Light a second candle to represent our respect for the young, maturing person you are right now.

Tween: (*Light second candle.*)

Parent(s): *Created by God* is a time for us to look ahead at the person you are becoming. It will be important for us to continue talking with one another about the important things happening to you and how they are shaping the adult you—even when the talking is difficult. Light a third candle to remind us that we will need the light of Christ to guide us together into the future when we will connect, adult to adult, and remember how this experience has strengthened that connection.

Tween: *(Light third candle.)*

Parent(s): As adults who care about you lead you through this experience, we will all be companions in the journey into and through this time of growing up. When you get to feeling lonely along the way, know that you are not alone. We love you, respect you, and want the best for you as you continue becoming the person God created you to be.

Tween: Thank you, God, for who I was, who I am, and who I am becoming; for parents, other adults, and friends who stand by me; and for Jesus, who went through all that I am and will be going through. In his name we pray.

All: Amen!

CPSIA information can be obtained at www.ICGtesting.com
Printed in the USA
LVOW08n0330060914

402670LV00001B/1/P